Dragon's Breath Publishing
Book Catalog

TIM CONLEY

ISBN: 1-5331-1571-0
ISBN-13: 978-1-5331-1571-3

DEDICATION

I would like to dedicate this book to my wife, Carmela and to my two children, Tanitha and James. They have all been very instrumental to my writing.

ACKNOWLEDGMENTS

I want to acknowledge Robert and Sloane Cheatham who gave me the idea to produce this book for the Pinelandia Art Gallery presentation of my books.

Catalog Items 1 & 2

The Curse of Indian Gold
Genre: Adventure/Horror
Published: 2006   Price: $7.99

A Time to Care
Prequel to The Curse of Indian Gold
Published: Pending   Price: $7.99

The Curse of Indian Gold was written to document a tale told by my Mother regarding an adventure that my Grandfather had when he and five of his friends invaded an Indian gravesite. They took almost 7 pounds of gold from the site and were cursed because they didn't put it back. Each was told how they would die – one year apart on the anniversary of the desecration. My Grandfather went insane but the others died as predicted. I inherited one of the nuggets that my Father carried with him until his death. It will never be spent.

A Time to Care is the prequel to The Curse of Indian Gold and is a frontier adventure story about my full-blood Indian princess Grandmother – Monamee, also known in white circles as Mary Alice Daniels. She was captured by the Shawnee early in life and had to endure many hardships as she grew older. Her most painful was when her son decided to vandalize an ancient Indian grave. She had to pronounce a curse on him and his friends that resulted in a lot of heartache for their community.

The Pleistocene Pig

Tim Conley

Dragon's Breath Publishing

**The Benoit
Investigative
Service**

Tim Conley

Dragon's Breath Publishing

Catalog Items 3 & 4

The Pleistocene Pig
Genre: Murder Mystery
Published: 2013   Price: $7.99

The Benoit Investigative Service
Murder Mystery
Published: 2014   Price: $7.99

There are currently four books in the Benoit Sagas. These tales started in the mind of a friend of mine named David Paffrath – a teacher in San Jose, California. David came up with the ideas and I did the ghostwriting.

The Pleistocene Pig is a story about FBI Agent Ronald Benoit who assembles a team to battle an ancient creature from a long dead era – that proved to be not so dead. He has to battle the creatures, a band of bad men and the FBI just to get his team to safety.

The Benoit Investigative Service is a follow-on tale after the Pleistocene Pig. Benoit was let go from the FBI because he wouldn't toe the party line. He takes his team with him and they investigate murders and bring bad guys to justice – Benoit style.

The D'lberville Bayou Murders

Tim Conley

Dragon's Breath Publishing

YOU WANT SOME OF THIS?

GO AHEAD, REPORT ME
WE'LL SEE WHO'LL BE AT YOUR FRONT STEPS

Crime Busting - Benoit Style

Tim Conley

Dragon's Breath Publishing

Catalog Items 5 & 6

The D'lberville Bayou Murders
Genre: Murder Mystery
Published: 2015   Price: $7.99

Crime Busting – Benoit Style
Murder Mystery
Published: Pending   Price: $7.99

The D'lberville Bayou Murders centers around Biloxi, Mississippi and involves Ronald Benoit and his team as they take on a crime family who likes raping and murdering young women.

Crime Busting – Benoit Style is still in the writing phase and should be available June 2016. Benoit finds his team pitted against crime bosses, crooked cops and twisted government officials as they try to find the source of a massive terror weapon in orbit above the Earth.

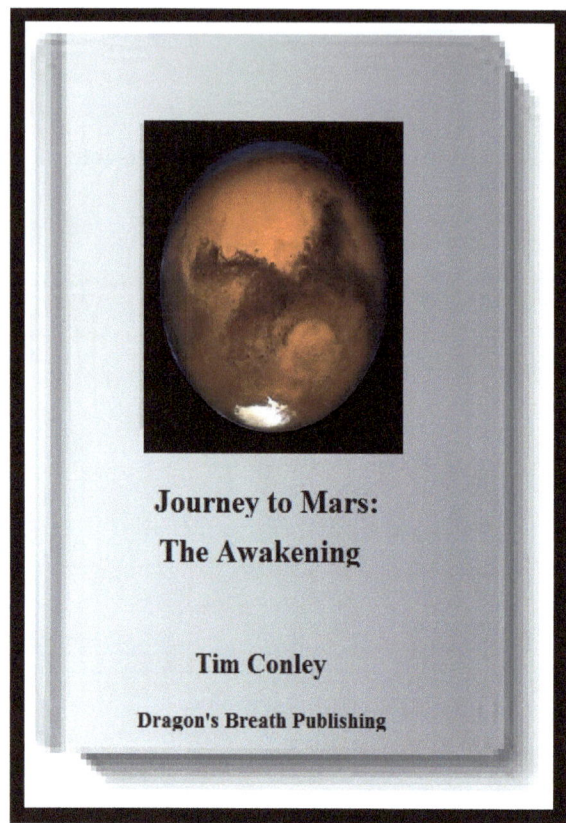

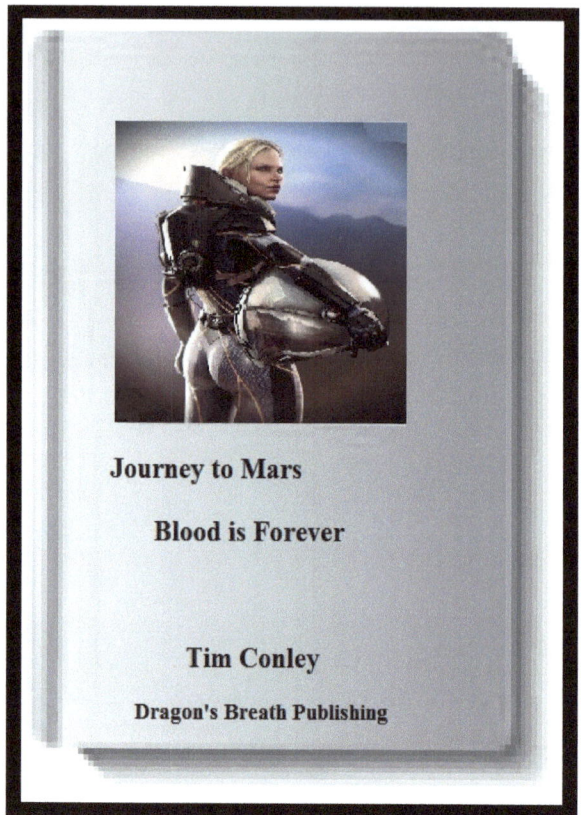

Catalog Items 7 & 8

Journey to Mars: The Awakening
Genre: Sci-fi Space Opera
Published: 2006   Price: $7.99

Journey to Mars: Blood is Forever
Sci-fi Space Opera
Published: 2007   Price: $7.99

Journey to Mars: The Awakening is the first book in a five book series that tells the story of Jason Martin and his crew who are on the third manned mission to Mars when they get hijacked by an ancient virus that turns some of his crew into vampires. He has to stop them from getting to Earth and fails as Marsella escapes and makes her way to Paris.

Blood is Forever takes up the tale twenty years on as Jason's daughter Catherine seeks ancient tech that could allow them to return to Earth. Meantime a foursome of friends have to battle Marsella until the cavalry arrives to turn the tide.

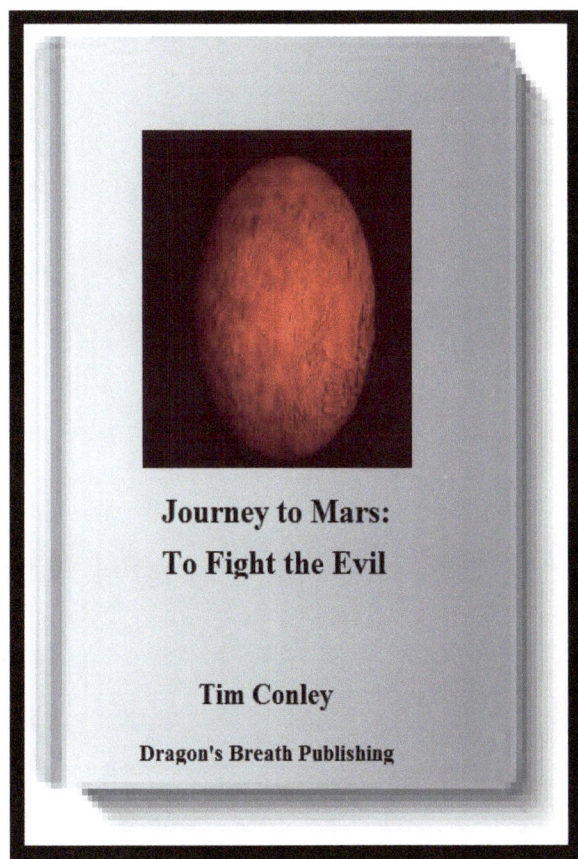

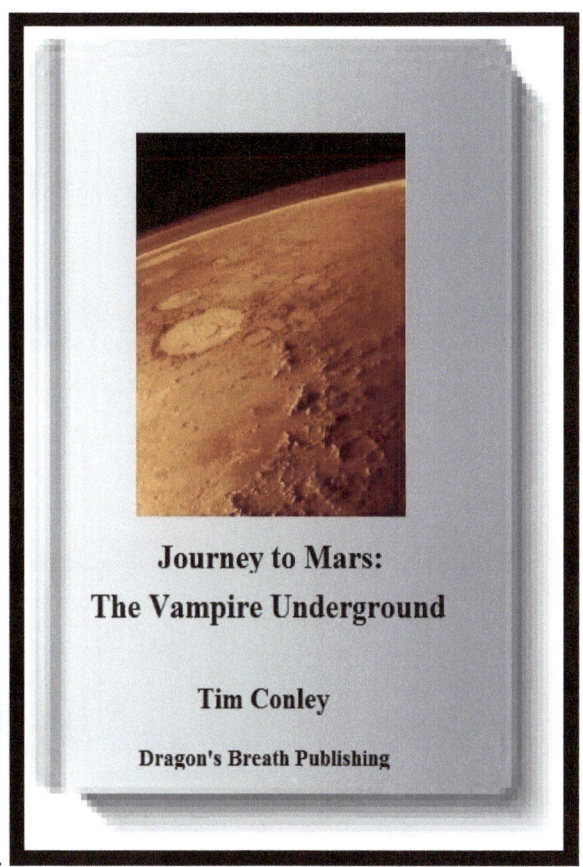

Catalog Items 9 & 10

Journey to Mars: To Fight the Evil
Genre: Sci-fi Space Opera
Published: 2007   Price: $7.99

Journey to Mars: The Vampire Underground
Sci-fi Space Opera
Published: 2009   Price: $7.99

Journey to Mars: To Fight the Evil and The Vampire Underground are the third and fourth in the series that pits Jason Martin and his friends in an all-out battle for Earth. They hang on by a thread as Marsella unleashes all the power she has in an effort to stay atop the food chain.

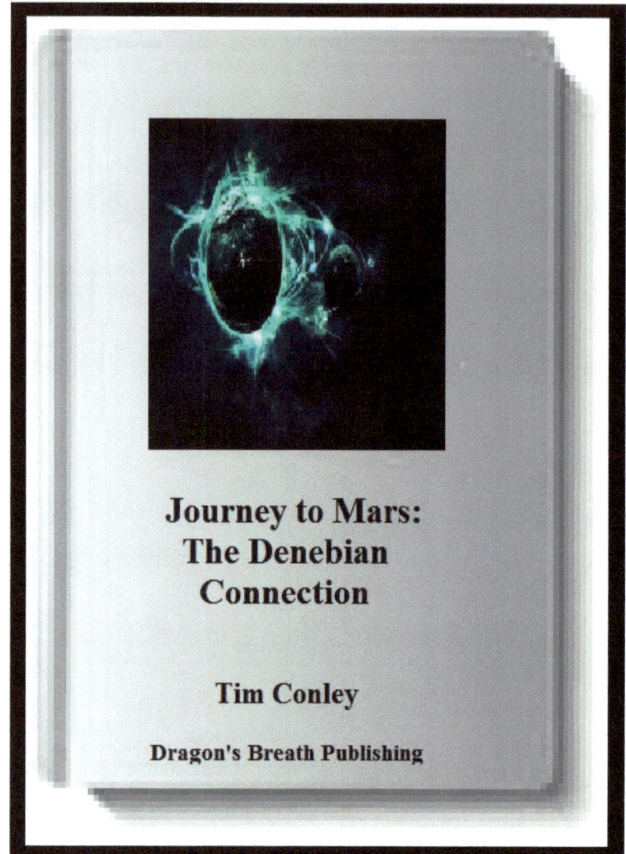

Catalog Items 11 & 12

Journey to Mars: The Denebian Connection
Genre: Sci-fi Space Opera
Published: Pending   Price: $7.99

The Guardians of Time:Opening Gambit
Sci-fi Adventure
Published: 2015   Price: $7.99

The Guardians of Time is a three volume saga that pits three siblings against the Puppet Masters of the Universe in a bid to determine who will control the Earth, the solar system and the galaxy. This is the brainchild of Carmela Santos – ghostwritten by Tim Conley.

The Guardians of Time: Middle Game

Tim Conley

Dragon's Breath Publishing

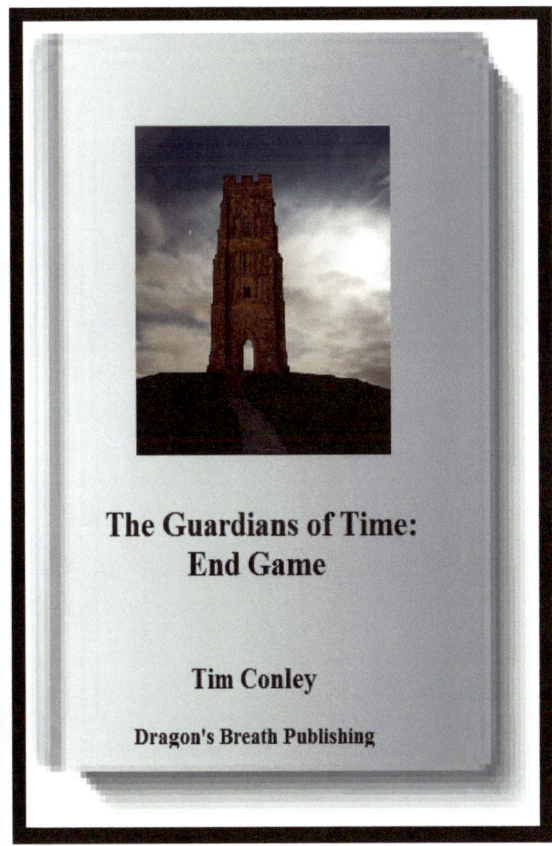

The Guardians of Time: End Game

Tim Conley

Dragon's Breath Publishing

Catalog Items 13 & 14

The Guardians of Time: Middle Game
Genre: Sci-fi Adventure
Published: Pending   Price: $7.99

The Guardians of Time: End Gambit
Sci-fi Adventure
Published: Pending   Price: $7.99

The Guardians of Time is a three volume saga that pits three siblings against the Puppet Masters of the Universe in a bid to determine who will control the Earth, the solar system and the galaxy. This is the brainchild of Carmela Santos – ghostwritten by Tim Conley.

Catalog Items 15 & 16

Crystal Possession: Vanessa's Story
Genre: Sci-fi Adventure
Published: 2010   Price: $7.99

Crystal Possession: Imagination Island
Sci-fi Adventure
Published: 2012   Price: $7.99

Crystal Possession is a two volume set that tells the story of Vanessa Keiling and her twin sister Ali. A crystal is discovered that contains an ancient entity from Atlantis. The priest inside the crystal tries to control the sisters and gain access into current day Earth. They have to stop him.

Catalog Items 17 & 18

Tales from Avalon
Genre: Sci-fi Adventure
Published: 2006   Price: $7.99

More Avalonian Tales
Sci-fi Adventure
Published: Pending   Price: $7.99

Tales from Avalon is a loose collection of stories that blend to tell how Earth might have been colonized. More Avalonian Tales takes up the saga in modern times – projecting what might become of our civilization.

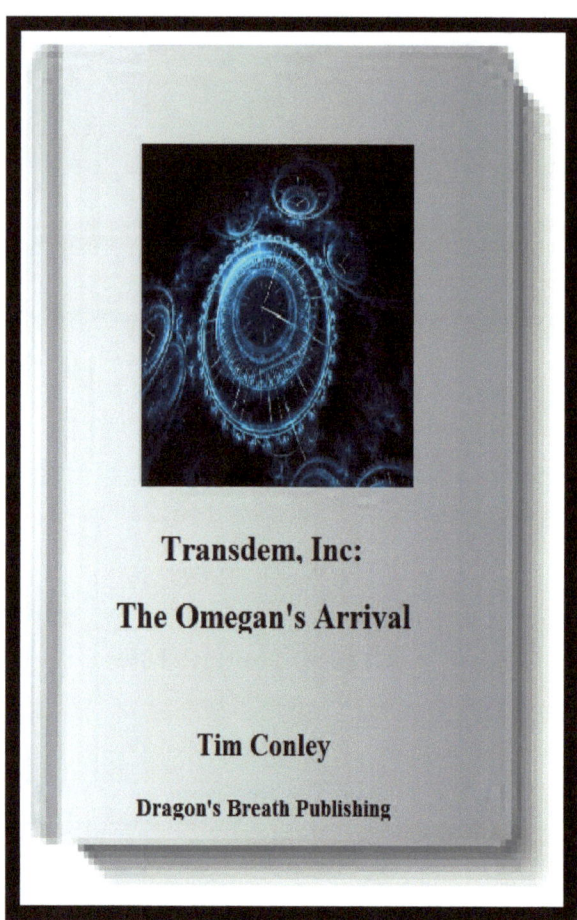

Catalog Items 19 & 20

Transdem, Inc: The Omegan's Arrival
Genre: Sci-fi Adventure
Published: 2007   Price: $7.99

Transdem, Inc: Escape into Elsewhere
Sci-fi Adventure
Published: Pending   Price: $7.99

Transdem, Inc. is a four volume set that tells of Martin Reiner – who, sitting in his den one night, sees his daughter, Lesa, and her cat, Pazee, walk out of a wall. He goes just slightly loopy and has to seek medical treatment while all along it is his destiny to save the Earth from invasion. Escape into Elsewhere documents what happens when they defeat one of the bad guys. The other one is in hot pursuit and time is not on Martin's side.

Catalog Items 21 & 22

Transdem, Inc: Saval's Revenge
Genre: Sci-fi Adventure
Published: Pending   Price: $7.99

Transdem, Inc: The Ends of the Universe
Sci-fi Adventure
Published: Pending   Price: $7.99

Transdem, Inc. is a four volume set that tells of Martin Reiner – who, sitting in his den one night, sees his daughter, Lesa, and her cat, Pazee, walk out of a wall. He goes just slightly loopy and has to seek medical treatment while all along it is his destiny to save the Earth from invasion. Escape into Elsewhere documents what happens when they defeat one of the bad guys. The other one is in hot pursuit and time is not on Martin's side.

Catalog Items 23 & 24

Dark Moons on Chimera: Birthright under a Sign:
Genre: Fantasy Adventure
Published: 2009   Price: $7.99

Dark Moons on Chimer: Adventures of Kn'Ross
Fantasy Adventure
Published: Pending   Price: $7.99

The Dark Moons/Rhumgold Sagas contains 9 volumes that deal with adventures centering in alien landscapes – dealing with witches, demons, vampires, large dogs and triplets born under a sign from aligned planets that bodes well for no one.

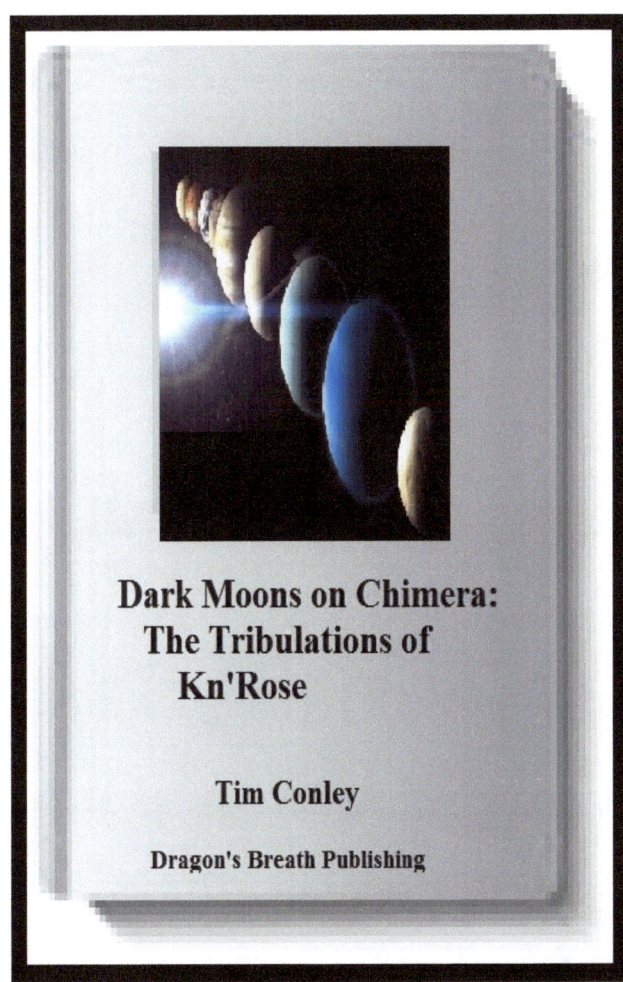

Catalog Items 25 & 26

Dark Moons on Chimera: Tribulations of Kn'Rose
Genre: Fantasy Adventure
Published: Pending   Price: $7.99

Triple Thrones of Theuniss
Fantasy Adventure
Published: 2016   Price: $7.99

The Dark Moons/Rhumgold Sagas contains 9 volumes that deal with adventures centering in alien landscapes – dealing with witches, demons, vampires, large dogs and triplets born under a sign from aligned planets that bodes well for no one.

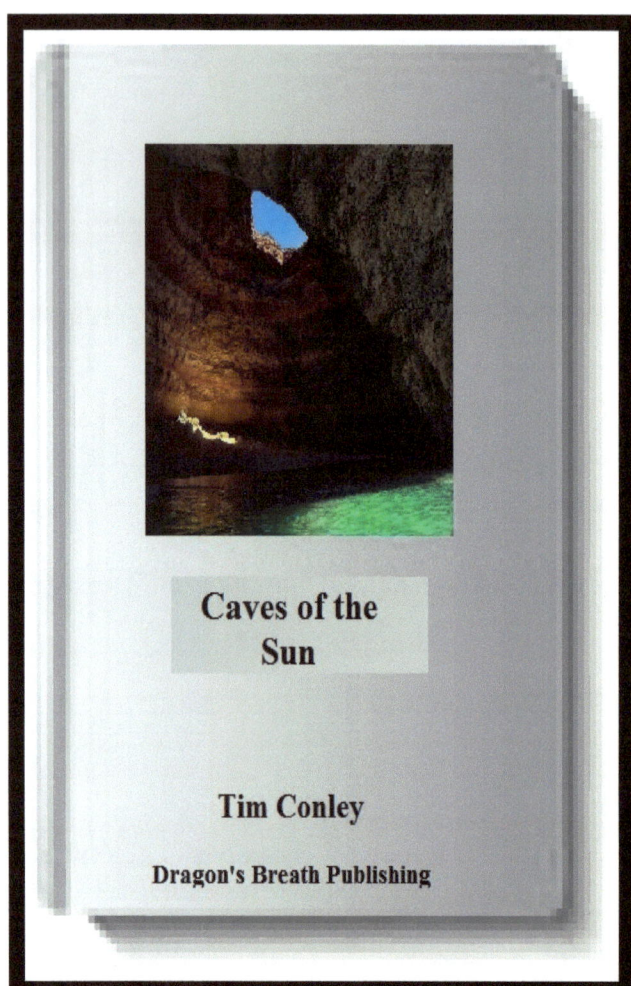

Caves of the Sun

Tim Conley

Dragon's Breath Publishing

Ysibol and the Dark Moons of Chimera

Tim Conley

Dragon's Breath Publishing

Catalog Items 27 & 28

Rhumgold Sagas: Caves of the Sun
Genre: Fantasy Adventure
Published: Pending   Price: $7.99

Ysibol and the Dark Moons of Chimera
Fantasy Adventure
Published: Pending   Price: $7.99

The Dark Moons/Rhumgold Sagas contains 9 volumes that deal with adventures centering in alien landscapes – dealing with witches, demons, vampires, large dogs and triplets born under a sign from aligned planets that bodes well for no one.

World Gates

Tim Conley

Dragon's Breath Publishing

The Witching Dimension

Tim Conley

Dragon's Breath Publishing

Catalog Items 29 & 30

Rhumgold Sagas: World Gates
Genre: Fantasy Adventure
Published: 2015   Price: $7.99

The Witching Dimension
Fantasy Adventure
Published: 2015   Price: $7.99

The Dark Moons/Rhumgold Sagas contains 9 volumes that deal with adventures centering in alien landscapes – dealing with witches, demons, vampires, large dogs and triplets born under a sign from aligned planets that bodes well for no one.

Catalog Items 31 & 32

Rhumgold Sagas: Under a Blood Moon
Genre: Fantasy Adventure
Published: Pending   Price: $7.99

Moon Base Alpha
Sci-fi Adventure
Published: Pending   Price: $7.99

Under a Blood Moon is a vampire/werewolf thriller that pits a double-dating foursome against denizens of the dark arts who decide to interrupt their necking session.

Moon Base Alpha is the brain child of Ron Davis which is being ghostwritten by Tim Conley.

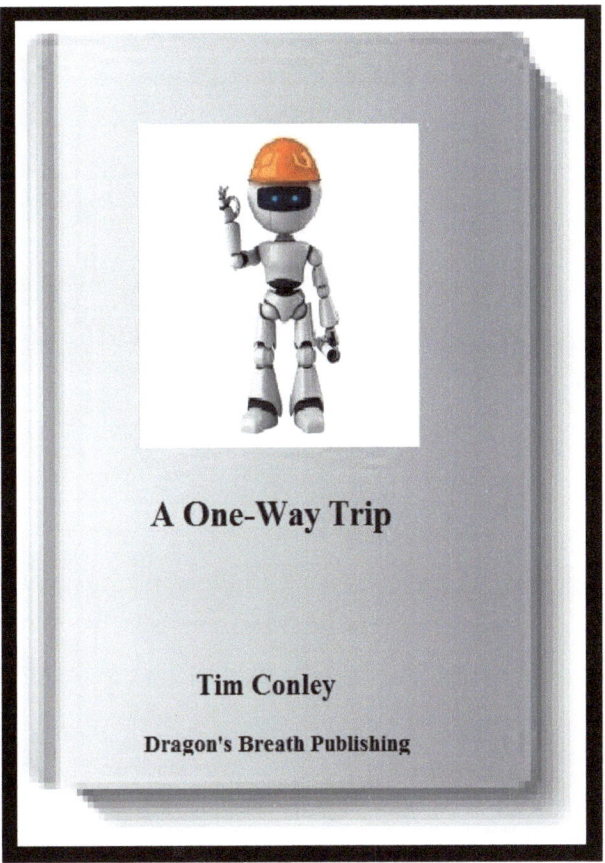

Catalog Items 33 & 34

Operation Arachnid: On High Alert
Genre: Murder Adventure
Published: 2015   Price: $7.99

A One-Way Trip
Sci-fi
Published: 2013   Price: $7.99

Operation Arachnid features a policeman who was critically wounded in the line of duty – nursed back to health by a covert organization who help him to fight crime.

A One-Way Trip follows a self-aware robot as he assists humans who are attempting to transfer to a base in the future to avoid a worldwide calamity.

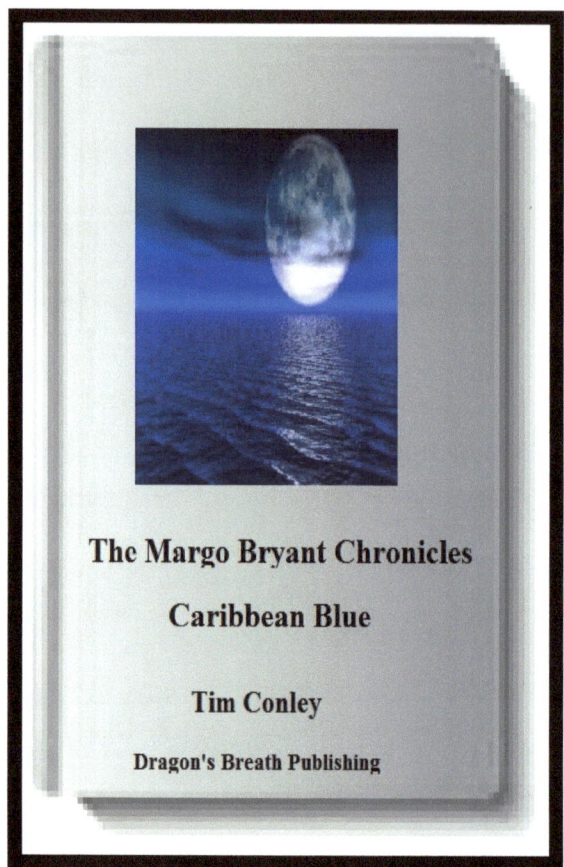

Catalog Items 35 & 36

Murder by Design
Genre: Murder Mystery
Published: 2012   Price: $7.99

The Margo Bryant Chronicles
Murder Mystery
Published: 2014   Price: $7.99

Murder by Design is a mystery story by David Paffrath – ghostwritten by Tim Conley.

Caribbean Blue is a Margo Bryant murder mystery/adventure set on St. Croix – near the Bahamas.

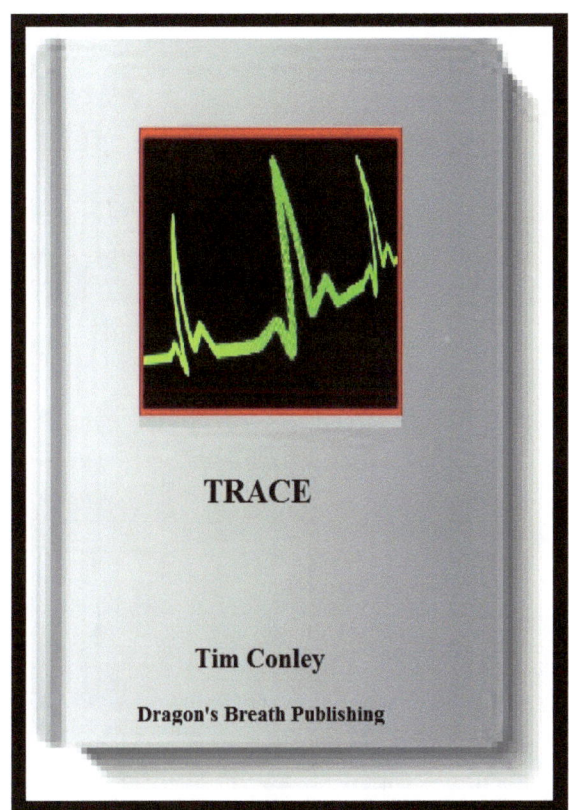

Catalog Items 37 & 38

TRACE
Genre: Murder Adventure
Published: 2015   Price: $7.99

Vampires R Us
Fantasy
Published: 2016   Price: $7.99

TRACE is about a company that wants to dominate the world by introducing nanites into breakfast cereal.

Vampires R Us is a tale in the Rhumgold Sagas that pits triplets in high adventure to defeat an ancient evil in another dimension.

    e.

Thunder Breaks In On Silence

Tim Conley

Dragon's Breath Publishing

Short Stories, Essays and Comments

Tim Conley

Dragon's Breath Publishing

Catalog Items 39 & 40

Thunder Breaks in on Silence
Genre: Fiction/Poetry
Published: 2012 Price: $7.99

Short Stories, Essays and Comments
Fiction
Published: 2013 Price: $7.99

Thunder Breaks in on Silence is a book of short stories and poetry.

Short Stories, Essays and Comments is a book of short stories and essays.

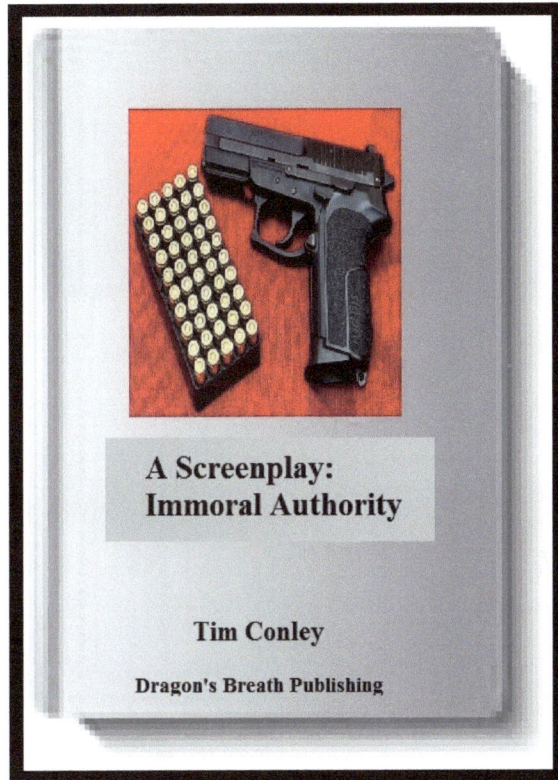

Catalog Items 41 & 42

Immoral Authority
Genre: Screenplay
Published: 2012   Price: $7.99

Joseph & Asseneth
Screenplay
Published: 2013   Price: $7.99

Immoral Authority is a tale about a VietNam vet who wants to live a quiet life but finds it interrupted by a comrade he thought dead. His family must pay for his past sins.

Joseph & Asseneth tells the story of the love affair between Joseph, son of Jacob, and Asseneth, daughter of the High Priest of On – in Egypt.

Catalog Items 43 & 44

Having your leg up on the Well
Genre: Fiction
Published: Pending   Price: $7.99

Wolfsden X at Sirius IV
Sci-fi
Published: Pending   Price: $7.99

Having your leg up on the Well is a satire that pokes fun at some of the things modern man considers important to our way of life.

Every 25 years a plague of warships comes buzzing across Earth. This time Earth must find the enemy and destroy it – else the planet will be stripped bare.

Catalog Items 45 & 46

Morgan la Fey and the Rings of Gold
Genre: Sci-fi
Published: Pending   Price: $7.99

The Primitive Shoppe
Sci-fi
Published: Pending   Price: $7.99

Morgan la Fey is different and that difference closes doors she thinks should have been open to her. She captures a fleet and holds Earth for ransom until the World Senate bends to reason.

A family at odds with each other stops at a roadside shack that turns out to be anything but normal. They each choose a different room and experience their own realities, but can they get back?

Catalog Items 47 & 48

Poetic License
Genre: Poetry
Published: 2010   Price: $7.99

Poetry from the heart.

A Poetic Life
Poetry
Published: 2014   Price: $7.99

Vintage poetry from the pen of Trudy Bonincontro.

Catalog Items 49 & 50

The First Shadow Rider
Genre: Fantasy
Published: 2014   Price: $7.99

The Shadow Returns
Fantasy
Published: 2015   Price: $7.99

The First Shadow Rider is a dragons and elves reunion that starts the three book saga of an elf's chances of riding her very own dragon. She bears the mark of the Shadow – which makes her powerful.

The Shadow Returns is the second installment of the series – written by Nicole Wendroth. The Shadow was briefly vanquished in the first book but has returned to wreck havoc.

Catalog Items 51 & 52

The Shadow's Betrayer
Genre: Fantasy
Published: Pending   Price: $7.99

Confessions of a Sex Addict
Erotic Fiction
Published: 2013   Price: $7.99

The Shadow's Betrayer finishes the story of a young girl and her dragon. They are betrayed by someone they considered a friend and must overcome the fallout of the event.

Confessions of a Sex Addict is a book by Amy Grant in which she tells all of the juicy details of her life as she lives to the hilt – so to speak.

Catalog Items 53 & 54

The Forensic Diaries
Genre: Teen Fiction
Published: 2014 Price: $7.99

Vira Sirium
Teen Fiction
Published: 2015 Price: $7.99

The Forensic Diaries is a story by Destiny Stone that details cases worked by a forensic scientist and her team.

Vira Sirium is a Teen Fiction by Destiny Stone that deals with how a family has to stick together to survive in a world that features non-human participants.

Catalog Items 55 & 56

EVOL LOVE
Genre: Teen Fiction
Published: 2014   Price: $7.99

Evolving Love
Teen Fiction
Published: 2015   Price: $7.99

EVOL LOVE is a Teen Fiction by Destiny Stone that deals with how a family has to stick together to survive in a world that features non-human participants.

Evolving Love is a Teen Fiction by Destiny Stone that deals with how a family has to stick together to survive in a world that features non-human participants.

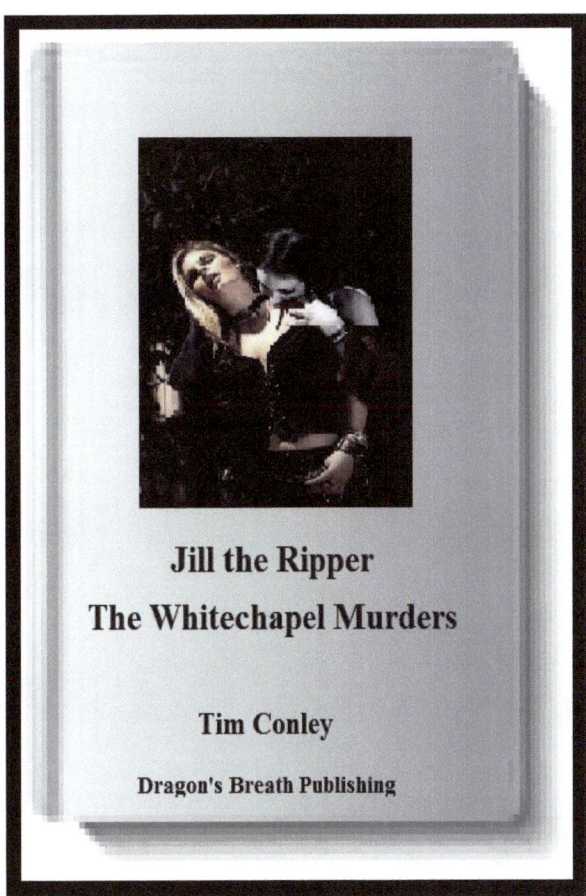

Catalog Items 57 & 58

Immoral Authority
Genre: Teen Fiction
Published: 2014   Price: $7.99

Jill the Ripper: The Whitechapel Murders
Horror Fiction
Published: Pending   Price: $7.99

A Day in the Life is a Teen Fiction by Destiny Stone that deals with how a family has to stick together to survive in a world that features non-human participants.

Jill the Ripper: The Whitechapel Murders is the brainchild of Carmela Conley and ghostwritten by her husband, Tim. It is possible that Scotland Yard was looking in the wrong direction for a killer.

Demographic Variables
and Self-Efficacy

Dr. Gertrude Bonincontro

Dragon's Breath Publishing

British Female
Travel Writers

Dr. Alison Day

Dragon's Breath Publishing

Catalog Items 59 & 60

Demographic Variables and Self-Efficacy
Genre: Doctoral Thesis
Published: 2012   Price: $7.99

British Female Travel Writers
Doctoral Thesis
Published: 2012   Price: $7.99

Dr. Trudy Bonincontro wrote her doctoral thesis as part of her effort to complete her degree. She deals with those factors that impact college students when they strive to work on degree requirements.

Dr. Alison Day documents the efforts of British travel writers on the Indian sub-continent during the late 1800's. She produced her thesis to satisfy requirements for her doctoral degree.

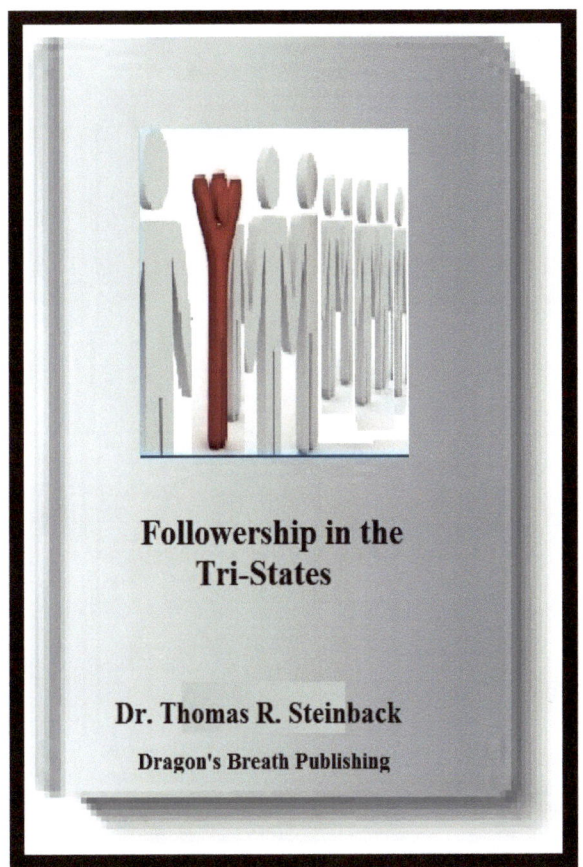

Followership in the Tri-States

Dr. Thomas R. Steinback

Dragon's Breath Publishing

Grandma Conley's Family

Tim Conley

Dragon's Breath Publishing

Catalog Items 61 & 62

Immoral Authority
Genre: Doctoral Thesis
Published: 2012   Price: $7.99

Grandma Conley's Family
Biography
Published: 2012   Price: $11.99

Dr. Thomas Steinback wrote his doctoral thesis to satisfy graduation requirements.

Mary Alice Conley was the Mother of 14, the Grandmother of 88 and Great-Grandmother of 14 – she was the matriarch of an extended family and was good at managing the family.

Catalog Items 63 & 64

The Life and Times of Ruth Yothers
Genre: Biography
Published: 2010   Price: $7.99

Mary Magdeline Exposed
Non-Fiction
Published: Pending   Price: $7.99

The Life and Times of Ruth Yothers is a biography that deals with the highlights of a modern woman who dedicated her life to her husband and family.

Mary Magdeline Exposed is an indepth look at a companion of Jesus of Nazareth. This book is non-fiction and uses parts of the Gospel of Mary to investigate her life.

Catalog Items 65 & 66

Greek/Hebrew Legacy
Genre: Student Guide
Published: Pending   Price: $11.99

Faith, Reason and Imagination
Student Guide
Published: Pending   Price: $11.99

Greek/Hebrew Legacy is a Study Guide produced for students in the course with the same name at the University of Memphis.

Faith, Reason and Imagination is a Study Guide produced for students in the course with the same name at the University of Memphis.

Catalog Items 67 & 68

Cloning: Am I Me?
Genre: Sci-fi
Published: Pending   Price: $7.99

The Age of Reason
Sci-fi
Published: Pending   Price: $7.99

Cloning: Am I Me? is about a man who discovers he might have been cloned when he meets his doppleganger on evening in a mall. He must trace his steps against those who want to silence him.

The Age of Reason is a sci-fi story about a man who is terrified of developing a mind debilitating disease that could diminish his creative capacity.

gematria

Tim Conley

Dragon's Breath Publishing

The Arclight Royale

Tim Conley

Dragon's Breath Publishing

Catalog Items 69 & 70

gematria
Genre: Sci-fi
Published: Pending   Price: $7.99

The Arclight Royale
Sci-fi
Published: Pending   Price: $7.99

gematria is a word that comes to us from ancient Iran and details a man's enterprises as he tries to save himself and members of his family from a drug cartel.

In The Arclight Royale the Earth is suddenly bombarded from space by the first group of aliens to make their presence known. Earth must fight back but the road to survival is bereft with many obstacles.

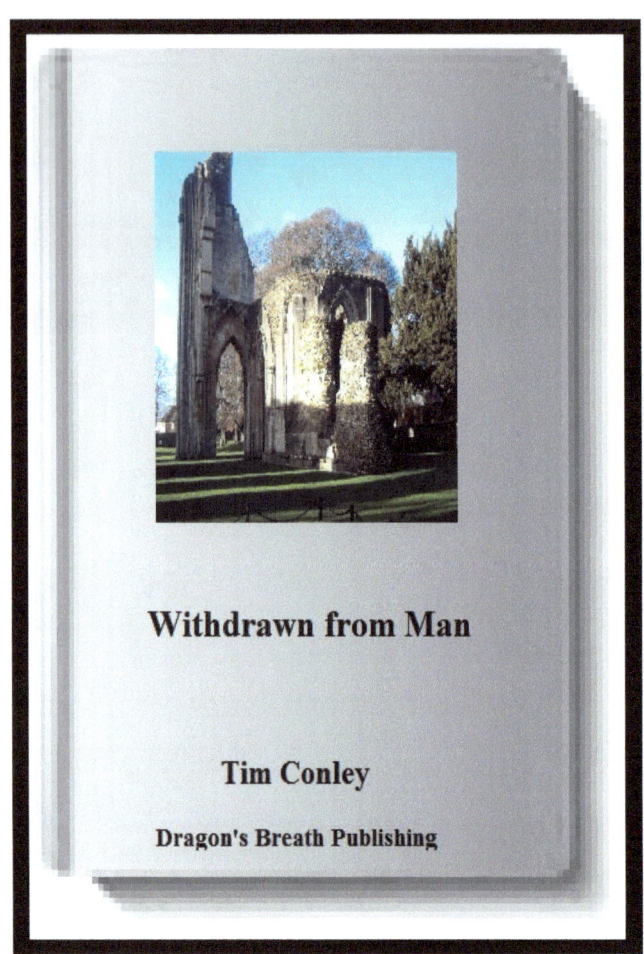

Catalog Items 71 & 72

Withdrawn from Man
Genre: Historical Fiction
Published: Pending   Price: $7.99

Bill Lundy's Last Roundup
Western
Published: Pending   Price: $7.99

Withdrawn from Man is a tale about a woman who tries to solve the mystery of the disappearance of a race that used to co-exist alongside man. She becomes a target.

Bill Lundy's Last Roundup is a Western about a man who is fast seeing his way of life disappear under his saddle. He must adjust to the changes that are coming fast.

Catalog Items 73 & 74

The Documentary Hypothesis
Genre: Religious
Published: Pending   Price: $7.99

A Commentary on II Timothy
Religious
Published: 2015   Price: $7.99

Is there "P" in the Bible was a thesis I wrote for a University course at Memphis State University in 1992. It tracks how the Hebrew Bible was constructed.

A Commentary on II Timothy is the product of James Conley. He wrote it while a student at the Memphis School of Preaching.

Catalog Items 75 & 76

Writing 101: For Beginners
Genre: How-To
Published: 2006   Price: $7.99

How to Write Fiction
How-To
Published: 2013   Price: $7.99

Writing 101 is a how-to book for those who want to begin writing. It has a lot of sage advice that novice writers can use to further their careers.

Zoey Nolen sent me a manuscript she had put together and asked that I publish it. In it she shows a lot of good examples of writing.

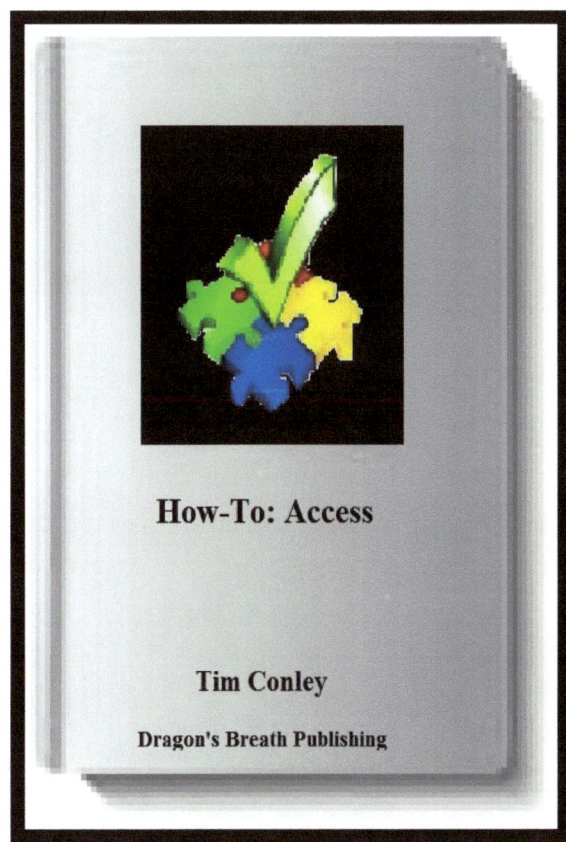

Catalog Items 77 & 78

How-to: Access
Genre: How-To
Published: 2011   Price: $7.99

How-to: Excel
How-To
Published: 2010   Price: $7.99

How-to: Access is a tutoring manual for my Microsoft Access students.

How-to: Excel is a tutoring manual for my Microsoft Excel students.

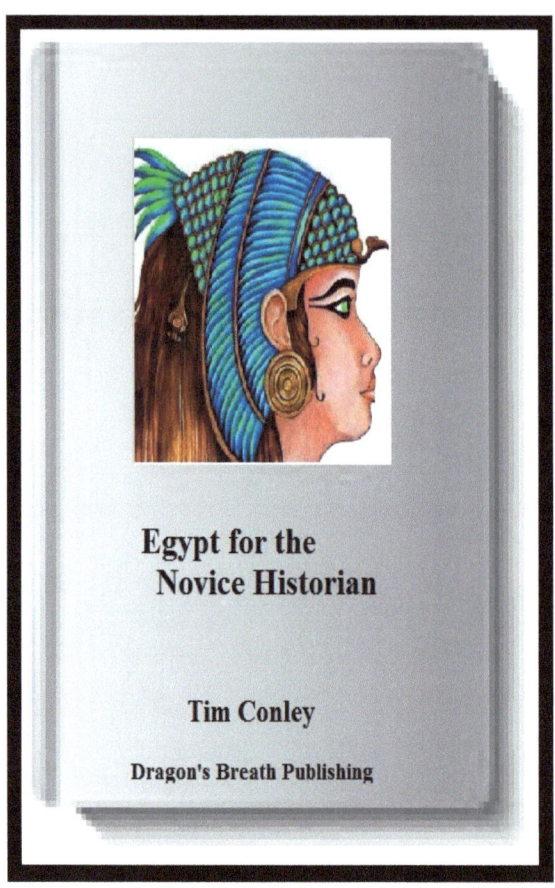

Catalog Items 79 & 80

Understanding Chess
Genre: How-To
Published: 2012 Price: $7.99

Egypt for the Novice Historian
Non-Fiction
Published: 2014 Price: $32.00

How-to: Chess is a tutoring manual for my Chess students.

Egypt for the Novice Historian is a non-fiction book written for my son, James, while he was in seminary school.

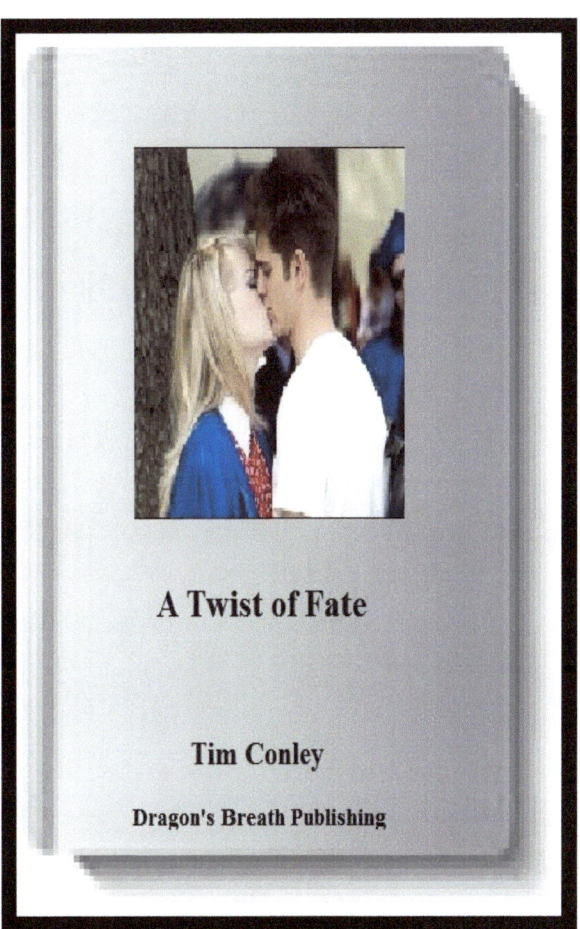

Catalog Items 81 & 82

Are You Afraid of Clowns
Genre: Non-Fiction
Published: 2015   Price: $7.99

A Twist of Fate
Murder Mystery
Published: Pending   Price: $7.99

Dennis Percy wrote a small non-fiction book that explores the world of clowns and the phobias that are sometimes associated with them.

A Twist of Fate comes from the mind of David Paffrath and is ghostwritten by Tim Conley.

Catalog Items 83 & 84

Till Death do us part
Genre: Murder Mystery
Published: Pending   Price: $7.99

In the Shadow of the Sword
Historical Fiction
Published: Pending   Price: $7.99

Till Death do us part is a murder mystery that begins when a husband and wife are kidnapped and have to strive to bring themselves back together.

In the Shadow of the Sword is a Civil War era fiction piece that pits our hero against his counterpart who is serving on the opposite side of the conflict and wants his girl.

Catalog Items 85 & 86

Hit Men Don't Make Good Daddies
Genre: Murder Mystery
Published: Pending   Price: $7.99

Tommyhawk
Murder Mystery
Published: Pending   Price: $7.99

Hit Men Don't Make Good Daddies is a murder mystery that centers around a man who is given the babies when his wife dies suddenly. He tries to juggle being a daddy and an assassin.

Tommyhawk is a murder mystery from the mind of David Paffrath and ghostwritten by Tim Conley.

Catalog Items 87 & 88

Escape from Jamestown
Genre: Historical Fiction
Published: Pending   Price: $7.99

It Won't be long now
Fiction
Published: Pending   Price: $7.99

Escape from Jamestown involves a young man who is mysteriously transported to Jamestown of the year 1779. He has to think fast in order to not give himself away as a warlock.

It Won't be long now investigates the 'End Days' as a lot of evangelicals like to call the time that we are living in.

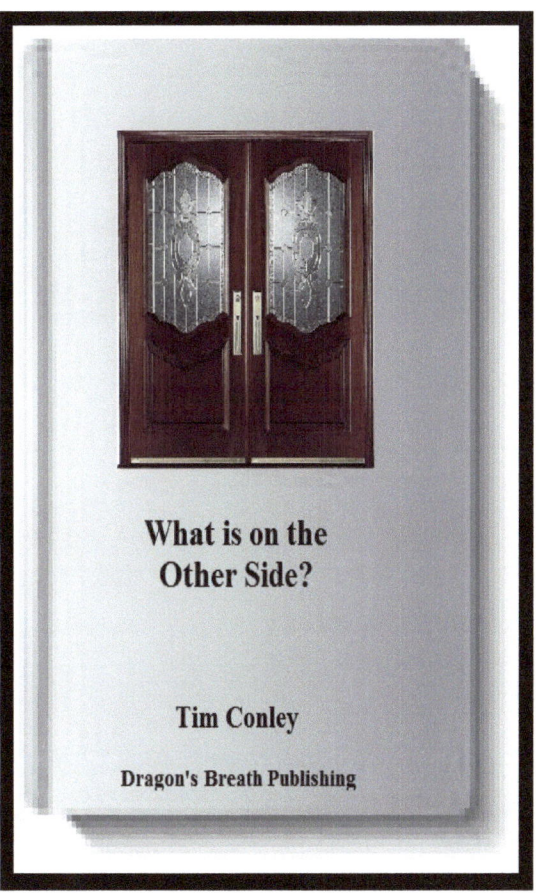

Catalog Items 89 & 90

How Did It Happen
Genre: Apocalyptic Fiction
Published: Pending   Price: $7.99

What is on the Other Side?
Non-Fiction
Published: Pending   Price: $7.99

How Did It Happen? tells the story of how world war III occurred and how mankind survived it.

What is on the Other Side? is a look at what happens when we die. Do we see the light or is there merely nothing between the here and now and eternity?

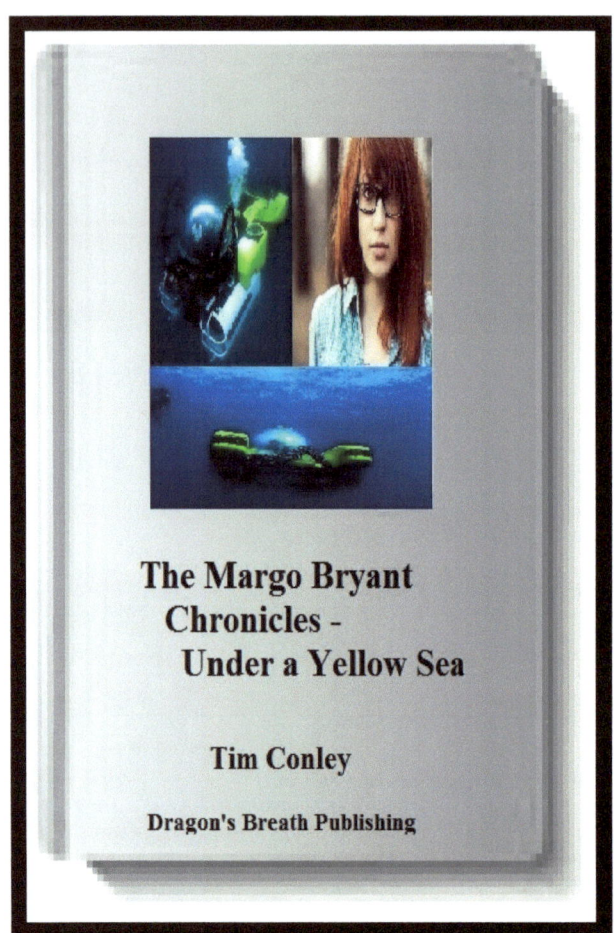

Catalog Items 91 & 92

Under a Yellow Sea
Genre: Murder Mystery
Published: Pending   Price: $7.99

The Red Pentagon
Murder Mystery
Published: Pending   Price: $7.99

Under a Yellow Sea is the second installment of the Margo Bryant Chronicles.

The Red Pentagon is the third installment of the Margo Bryant Chronicles.

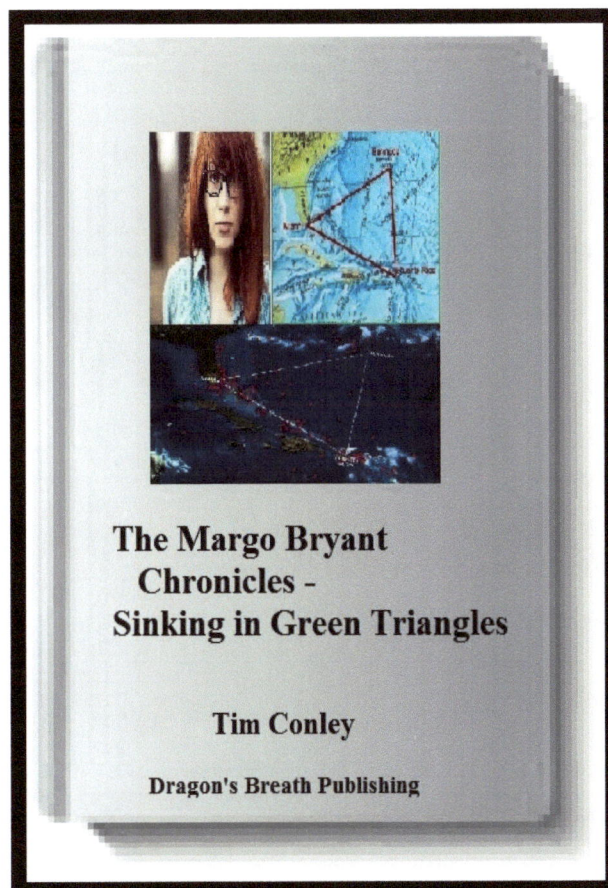

Catalog Items 93 & 94

Sinking in Green Triangles
Genre: Murder Mystery
Published: Pending   Price: $7.99

The Case of Black Death
Murder Mystery
Published: Pending   Price: $7.99

Sinking in Green Triangles is the fourth installment of the Margo Bryant Chronicles.

The Case of Black Death is the fifth installment of the Margo Bryant Chronicles.

Catalog Items 95 & 96

The White Chill
Genre: Murder Mystery
Published: Pending   Price: $7.99

Teddy Saves the Day
Children's Book
Published: 2014   Price: $7.99

The White Chill is the sixth installment of the Margo Bryant Chronicles.

Teddy Saves the Day is a small Children's Book.

ABOUT THE AUTHOR

Tim Conley really began writing at the young age of six when he would recount his daydreams to whoever would listen. His authoritarian father discouraged this and any other action that smelled of books and reading. Tim would sneak into any hidden away corner and escape through the avenue of reading and was known as a loner and dreamer by his classmates, preferring his own company and that of 'made-up characters' to that of friends. Now at age 66, Tim has a huge amount of material to draw from to create his own settings and characters.

Tim is still a loner, living with his wife and lover, Carmela Santos (a teacher from the Philippines). He would like to run a small ranch with a couple horses, some pigs and chickens.

Tim is satisfied to live the quiet life of a simple man. He studied writing at the University College at Memphis State University. The fact is he enjoys writing more than all the other things he has accomplished in life.

Teaching for inner city schools has provided excitement in his life, but he has configured a quiet place where he can sit at the computer during the evening to recount his 'thoughts of the day...dream.'

Tim has published over 40 books so far. He is an accomplished ghostwriter – having published story lines for David Paffrath and Ron Davis. He has also published three doctoral theses and recently added two new faces: Destiny Stone and Nicole Wendroth to his list of published individuals.

The following listing are books that have been published by Dragon's Breath Publishing or are currently in the pipeline to be published. They can be purchased by visiting www.dbponline.net and clicking on the links for each desired book. Paperback books can be ordered directly from Amazon.com and e-Books from Kindle Direct. Read & Enjoy!

Sci-fi category:
Transdem, Inc.
  The Omegan's Arrival
  Escape into Elsewhere
  Saval's Revenge
  The Ends of the Universe
Crystal Possession
  Vanessa's Story
  Imagination Island
Journey to Mars
  The Awakening
  Blood is Forever
  To Fight the Evil
  The Vampire Underground
  The Denebian Connection

Tales from Avalon
  Avalon, Book 1 – The Avalonian Connection
  Avalon, Book 2 – Genesis: To Outrun a Nova
  Avalon, Book 3 – The Toltec Expedition
  Avalon, Book 4 – The Chen Lao Conspiracy
  Avalon, Book 5 – The Oludavi Revelation
  Avalon, Book 6 – 2013: The Melting Pot
  Avalon, Book 7 – 2023: Life Here After
More Avalonian Tales
Cloning: Am I Me?
Operation Archnid: On High Alert
Wolfsden X at Sirius IV
Arclight Royal
Trace
gematria
A One-Way Trip (Tim Conley & Ron Davis)
Moon Base Alpha (Tim Conley & Ron Davis)
The Time Guardians
  Opening Gambit
  Middle Game
  End Game

Horror category:
The Curse of Indian Gold
A Time to Care
A Tale of Cardiff Glen
Jill: The Ripper
Pleistocene Pig (David Paffrath)

Fantasy:
Dark Moons on Chimera
  Birth under a Sign
  The Adventures of Kn'Ross
  The Tribulations of Kn'Rose
  The Triple Thrones of Theuniss
The First Shadow Rider (Nicole Wendroth)
The Shadow Returns (Nicole Wendroth)
The Shadow's Betrayer (Nicole Wendroth)
Vampire Investigative Service: Vampires R Us

Caves of the Sun

Biography/Poetry category:
Memoirs of a Country boy
Poetic License
Thunder Breaks in on Silence
Short Stories, Essays and Comments
A Poetic Life (Trudy Bonincontro)

How-to category:
Writing 101: For Beginners
How to Write Fiction
How to Repair Old Computers
How to Play Chess
How to: Access
How to: Excel
How-to: Dreamweaver8
How-to: HTML5
How-to: Powerpoint
How-to: Publish on CreateSpace
How-to: Publish on Kindle Direct

Screenplays:
A Screenplay: Immoral Authority
A Screenplay: Joseph & Asseneth

Murder Mystery
Murder by Design (David Paffrath)
The Margo Bryant Chronicles:
  Caribbean Blue
  Under a Yellow Sea
  The Red Pentagon
  Sinking in Green Triangles
  The Case of the Black Death
  The White Chill
The Benoit Investigative Service (David Paffrath)
The D'lberville Bayou Murders (David Paffrath)
Tommyhawk (David Paffrath)
A Twisted Fate (David Paffrath
Hit Men don't make good Daddys

Erotica
Confessions of a Sex Addict (Amy Grant)

Doctoral Thesis
British Female Travel Writers   (Alison Day)
Demographic Variables in Self-Efficacy in University Courses   (Trudy Bonincontro)
Followership in the Tri-States   (Thomas Steinback)

Historical Fiction
Withdrawn from Man
In the Shadow of the Sword
Escape from Jamestown

Till Death do us part

Children's Books
Teddy Saves the Day

Young Adventure
EVOL LOVE (Destiny Stone)
Evolving Love (Destiny Stone)
Vira Sirium (Destiny Stone)
A Day in the Life (Destiny Stone)
Forensic Diaries (Destiny Stone)

Religious/Societal Commentary
The Documentary Hypothesis
How did it happen?
It won't be long now
Having your feet upon the well
The Epistle of III Timothy
Thunder Breaks in on Silence
Short Stories, Essays and Comments
Egypt for the Novice Historian
What is on the other side?

Non-Fiction
Are you afraid of Clowns?

Biographies
The Life and Times of Ruth Yothers
Grandma Conley's Family: A Historical Reference